The Pocket Guide to Responsive Fundraising

28 Ways to Execute The Responsive Framework and Why It Matters

Gabe Cooper | Virtuous

Printed by Liberalis, in the United States of America.

First printing, 2019.

www.virtuouscrm.com

Contents

Introduction
We Have A Problem

We are in the middle of a generosity crisis.

Despite growing annual revenue, nonprofits are finding it increasingly difficult to inspire generosity from individual donors. Year after year, individuals give less to organizations in every vertical.

The result is a 25% decline in the number of low and mid-tier donors in the last decade. Now, this doesn't mean people are losing interest in giving. Quite the opposite, in fact. It turns out that people are more aware than ever before about the causes that need attention.

The problem is with how nonprofits connect with their supporters who desperately want to get closer to the cause.

The strategies that fundraisers have been using with a degree of reliable success, are now failing to resonate with donors in the way they had in the past.

Today's donors expect more from the organizations they support. They want to be included and informed about the meaningful work they are giving to.

In short, donors giving even as little as $100 want to be treated in the same kinds of ways major donors get treated. What's more, they will move away from nonprofits that fail to do this and toward those nonprofits that do.

Unfortunately, nonprofits aren't equipped to meet this new challenge. So, rather than adapt to meet the new standards of modern donors, fundraisers have been turning their attention to major-gift donors, where their development strategies work.

Nonprofits looking to grow in the next 5 years cannot afford to ignore the demands of the modern donor any longer. Your organization must evolve to focus on a more personalized development strategy that puts each donor at the center of your efforts.

You must embrace experimentation, change and sometimes even failure.

You need to dedicate yourself to responsive fundraising in order to inspire generosity from the modern donor.

Chapter 1:
The Evolution of Modern Donors

Until recently, the evolution of donors occurred slowly. In general, nonprofits were able to adapt to the new expectations and trends using existing resources. They could improve tactics by adding a little more staff time and expanding their tech stack. Subtle shifts in strategy were enough to appease donors and grow generosity.

But in the last 5 years, expectations have evolved at an exponential rate. Now, even the most agile nonprofits struggle to find meaningful ways to engage the modern donor.

At a macro level, we see a pair of specific changes that add to the velocity of this evolution.

First, attention is fractured. Large events and broadcast-style communication that used to capture the attention of large groups across the country no longer have the same power over our collective society. Outside of professional sports, the shared experience of broadcast media is nearly gone.

Instead, individuals stream entertainment on their own schedule, choose their own news sources and curate their own media experiences.

Your donors live in a world that is almost completely personalized to their tastes and preferences. This means that they curate the content your organization produces in the same way.

That curation wouldn't be possible without the second macro trend. Technology advanced in a way that enabled companies to leverage behavioral data to create better, more relevant customer experiences.

Without the promise of undivided attention, brands had to find a way to keep individuals engaged with their products and services. That meant giving everyone, each individual, the personalized experience they wanted.

Facebook, Netflix and Amazon are three of the most popular examples, using data to cater to the individual needs of a combined total of 594 million users.

More recently, less dominant companies like Stitch Fix applied this to fashion, Spotify to music, and Chewy to pet supplies. Each have grown customer adoption and loyalty through treating people less like segments and more like people.

As more and more organizations adopted a customer-centric approach, people realized what was possible, and quickly began to expect transparent, personalized experiences everywhere.

Modern donors expected authentic engagements with the causes they supported. They were no longer happy opening the same direct mail piece their neighbor received. Today, the supporters who care about your cause (and are most likely to give more than one time) want to be included in your mission.

Donors need proof that they are part of your success and not simply another name in your contact list. Nonprofits have no choice but to adapt or risk stifling their growth. And they must do it immediately.

We're already seeing the stifled growth. From 2006 to 2015, there was an 18% drop in the number of individuals who chose to give to nonprofits.

According to The Fundraising Effectiveness Project, nonprofits lose more than half of their donors each year, with 76% of new donors never giving again. But major gift donors? They continue to be a constant source of reliable fundraising.

The difference lies in the way nonprofits treat major gift donors.

Nonprofits have perfected the art of building relationships with major donors. Personal connections flourish. With good reason: there's a high return on investment on those relationships, so nonprofits can devote their time and resources to growing those few sustaining relationships. But they do so at the expense of every other relationship in their donor database.

The everyday givers are left with impersonal, unresponsive tactics. Fundraising to this segment is reduced to a numbers game, which is a terrible replacement for relationship-building. Every donor deserves a relationship with the causes they support.

To treat them as a number pushes the modern donor away and dramatically reduces (if not eliminates) the chances of them ever giving more than once.

The problem isn't just a strained relationship — it's the degradation of trust between individual donors and the nonprofits. The more you treat them like a number, the more they see you as another institution that is only interested in their money. And in our age of choice and information overload, trust is the most valuable asset in terms of loyalty, commitment and generosity.

Accenture reports that, "Poor personalization and lack of trust costs US organizations $756 billion last year, as 41 percent of consumers switched companies." Give.org reports that trust in nonprofit organizations decreased by 16% between 2017 and 2018.

The negative impacts of being unresponsive to your donors' needs will not slow down any time soon.

Instead of continuing to compromise growth and impact with strategies that aren't designed to build trusted relationships with today's donor, nonprofits need to rethink the entire model to mirror what they know works. In short, nonprofits need to treat every donor like a major donor.

Nonprofits need responsive fundraising.

Chapter 2:

Responsive Fundraising: The Answer to Modern Donors' Expectations

Responsive fundraising puts the donor at the center of your fundraising. Rather than focus on your organizational needs or the statistics about why your work is so important, the donor's needs are the driving force. Generosity grows through personalization of the donor journey, where each engagement brings the donor closer to the cause.

Remember: generosity is a deeply personal act. Most often, giving starts with a relationship. Someone was moved by the living conditions of a friendly tour guide they met in another country during their summer vacation. A loved one beat a rare disease despite little research. The rival school of someone's alma mater upgraded their library. Their child was bullied, and they want to see the problem eradicated. Regardless of the reason, it starts with a personal connection.

Responsive fundraising builds on that relational connection; it doesn't exploit it. Responsive nonprofits provide donors with relevant information to elicit a commitment to the work, beyond their personal story. A few questions to ask yourself if you were hoping to implement the responsive fundraising model are:

• What stage of life is this person in? How does that affect their generosity?

• What interested them in your cause the first time they gave? Has anything changed?

• What does your nonprofit know about their passions, interests, talents and experience?

• Where are they in the donor journey?

• What do they want to know about you? Have you found a good way of

• In what ways do they engage with your nonprofit? Are there any channels we aren't monitoring that they may be using to talk about our organization?

• When was the last time you gave back to the donor? Are you matching their passions with your cause?

- Do your donors naturally create communities around your cause? Can you connect them with other like-minded donors in your network?

- What is the next best step for them?

The answers to these questions will reveal paths to reach your donors in a more purposeful way. If the answers sound too simple, that shouldn't surprise you. Responsive fundraising strategies mimic the steps we all take to create lasting relationships with everyone in our lives. From siblings to spouses, each meaningful relationship we have follows a similar pattern.

First, we listen to learn details that aren't obvious. Next, we consider what we've learned and use that knowledge to connect in a meaningful way. Finally, we share a new experience based on all the new information. Successful relationships are a never-ending cycle of learning new things, contextualizing it and responding in a way that proves we not only understand, but also care deeply.

It's worked for families and friends for centuries, and it works with your modern donors.

The Responsive Framework

While the fundamental functions of relationship may seem obvious in your personal life, it makes sense that those same functions would seem too complicated for your organization to execute at scale. After all, how can you truly engage in a relational way thousands of contacts in your donor database? Here's everything you need to know about The Responsive Framework.

Listen

Responsive fundraising begins with listening. Of all 3 steps, this is perhaps the most counter-intuitive one, but also the most important.

The current state of marketing and fundraising for nonprofits posits that organizations should send the same information to the same people more often in the hopes of squeezing just a little more from the base. But as we've mentioned, and we all know, that doesn't work (at least it's not going to continue to work). Listening first is the radical change you need to see different results.

Listening to donors involves using the same behavior-based data insights that created the modern donor in the first place. Of course, you can always listen during in-person conversations or on the phone. But the most scalable way to listen to each individual donor's needs is to gather data and pull insights.

Leverage all available data to reach a comprehensive understanding of what each donor cares about, what they currently feel about your nonprofit and the best way to motivate them into their next act of generosity. Common ways you can listen to donors for signals about their interests and preferences include:

• **Website Forms** - Don't just rely on donation forms to listen for donor feedback. Drive new traffic to landing pages with gated white papers and long-form videos that can indicate what initiatives they're most interested in. Gather information about people before they even give for the first time.

• **Social Platforms** - Listen to how your constituents talk about your organization, both directly and indirectly. Notice what influencers they engage with. Look for the connections between their followers and other donors in your organization.

- **RFM Metrics** - Always have an up-to-date understanding of each donor's RFM (recency, frequency, monetary value) data so that you can tailor your suggestions to their current feelings towards your nonprofit and the work you do.

- **Content Engagement** - Track donors engagement metrics whenever possible. Look for trends in their behavior and opportunities to introduce new programs or connection opportunities.

As with all data-driven insights, the more you know, the faster you can act. Loyalty, advocacy and generosity will all happen faster because you have a full picture of both the work your nonprofit is doing and the ways it will resonate with each donor.

Connect

If listening is the most drastic change from past fundraising strategies, connecting is the most important change. Connection is what transforms you into a donor-centric, responsive nonprofit. Regardless of the channel or medium you use to communicate with donors, you have all the information you need to appeal to the desires and passions of donors directly.

Think about direct response fundraising tactics of the past. A fundraiser would mail a broad appeal to their entire contact list asking everyone to give the same exact way. The information might resonate with a few, but there was no useful way to validate why. The response to each appeal continues to be shockingly low. The only way to make up for that low response was to increase the frequency of the appeal. Most nonprofits continue this same process year after year, despite lackluster results.

The issue is the nonprofit is not building a relationship with their constituents. They're barely having a conversation. They say the same thing to the same people and hope to see different results. The only thing that changed was the rate at which they were alienating donors and losing individuals from their network.

On the other hand, with responsive fundraising tactics, you meet each donor where they are and you work to create the right message by learning about what they want, what they need, what they respond to. The connection deepens with each engagement because the conversation evolves. Every touchpoint is new, different and valuable to the modern donor because you took the time to personalize your message for them. A deep, relational connection results in a commitment to your cause.

Modern donors who feel included in your work will do what they can to make sure you succeed because they believe in what you're doing, and they will recognize that their generosity is moving the needle.

Suggest

The third part of the responsive fundraising cycle is suggesting the next best action. By intentionally building trust with the modern donor, and listening to their subtle and obvious signals, your organization can be more strategic about the generosity requests.

Knowing that your donors are capable of a variety of modes of generosity, your team can differentiate between when to recommend a monetary donation, and when a donor would prefer to give time or advice or when they can simply spread the word. Any suggestion to your donor will, in this case, be the result of an understanding of what your donors want to do in support of your cause.

It's important to note that it is not enough to only adopt the Listen and Connect portions and then suggest the same giving opportunity as before. You won't be a responsive fundraiser if you exclude the Suggest step. It helps to look beyond your immediate needs and see these donor relationships as ever-evolving. If your data directs you to hold off on a donation request and encourage a video view instead, you should be diligent about following the data. Even if it is late in December and you aren't on target to reach your goals.

Why? Because you wouldn't risk injuring your relationship with a major donor by making an ask that's out of sync with their relationship with you, so it's time to start thinking the same way about your everyday donors. The long play is that they, too, will give more over the course of their relationship when they're more engaged.

Remember, you are building a culture of responsive behavior. You are cultivating donor relationships that will extend beyond the first gift. Committing to the responsive fundraising framework means that you won't be part of the group who loses 76% of first-time donors. Your process is different because it prioritizes longevity, donor relationships and meaningful engagements that grow your organization.

The Technology You Need To Be Responsive

Responsive fundraising relies on the smart use of technology, not a ton of individual actions. Personalized donor journeys are created with data and automation. To be responsive, you need technology to support you. Here are the three most important tools to equip your team with in order to be a responsive nonprofit.

1. Responsive CRM

To be an efficient, responsive nonprofit, you need a CRM that serves your needs. Rather than an organization system, your nonprofit CRM should be a tool that makes your job easier.

A responsive CRM like Virtuous uses data to craft comprehensive donor profiles, robust reporting, engagement tracking, and predictive recommendations. It can signal when to make your next ask, identify your most important contacts to call, and even score your contacts based on social and wealth data.

The right CRM software will alleviate the demands on your team members, not add complexity to their daily responsibilities. Here are some of the benefits you will see right away when using a responsive CRM for your fundraising.

Increased Donor Retention and LTV

Donor retention is an important piece of your overall fundraising strategy. Most often, the cost of finding brand new potential donors and nurturing them through the entire journey is much higher than motivating a first time donor to give a second time.

A nonprofit CRM will help you engage with all your donors the right way. You can provide the information they want to know at the exact moment they are most interested. A data-driven CRM can create smart suggestions based on individual donor signals, plus the historical data of similar donors from the past.

What all this personalized, data-driven communication amounts to is higher donor satisfaction. Your base feels included, informed and important. Those emotions inspire loyalty, retention and an overall increase in lifetime value.

Improved Capacity for Employees

Capacity is an essential measurement of how your nonprofit can grow and scale in the future. A responsive CRM can improve your current capacity without hindering your growth in the future.

To see the need in your organization for a powerful nonprofit CRM, try to identify the ROI for your team's capacity. Put together all the daily, weekly and monthly tasks your team completes, plus the hours spent, and calculate how much time can be saved through automation and streamlined data collection.

Build extra enthusiasm from your team with a plan for what initiatives you want to work on with these new hours.

Faster Time to Generosity from Potential Donors

Managing donor relationships with an outdated CRM (or worse, manually) is a gigantic task that involves a number of steps and departments. Many nonprofits are all too familiar with the pain of a late thank you letter or a missed anniversary. Now, imagine adding in the task of nurturing your potential donors too. It would be impossible.

But recruiting and converting new contacts into donors is an essential part of your nonprofit's growth. To understand the impact a responsive CRM can make on your current growth trends, look at how well you're currently converting website traffic into donors, then give an estimate of the time it takes to make the conversion.

Next, establish a projection for how this conversion rate might increase with a powerful CRM. Both the rate and the time it takes to make the conversion are important metrics in making your marketing and development efforts more efficient.

2. Marketing Automation

The second essential addition to your suite of responsive software is a marketing automation tool. With marketing automation your supporters get the right communication at the right time, based on their preferences or behavior.

You create workflows with automatic actions, assign them to dynamic queries that are constantly updated with new donor behavior, and trigger next best actions with supporters based on engagement strategies you've created.

Automation makes it easier to connect with donors in a meaningful way on a regular basis, without spending all your time doing so. Emails, mail, social media and calls can all be executed automatically, giving your team space to do the big-picture thinking necessary to create deeper connections and inspire greater generosity.

Speaking of ROI, you want to know what we hear the most from fundraising leadership? Their biggest challenge is lack of efficiency. They are bogged down by hurdles in the technology they've adopted, systems often don't work well together, it's hard to make sense of the data, et cetera.

But inefficiency is not exclusively a technology problem. It has a lot to do with staffing. Communication channels are clogged, there's unnecessary redundancy in roles — and many teams are stuck doing manual work that for-profit companies have long since automated.

Not to mention that inefficiency has a cost that donors care about. Should organizations be expected to run on a skeleton crew and still be successful? No, but donors don't want you to waste your time or their money, so whenever you can improve efficiency, everyone wins.

Of course, we also hear that CDO's want to grow. They want to build meaningful relationships with their donors so that they can keep them in the ecosystem. This is where many emphasize that human fundraisers are important: the more we can create a personalized, direct connection to each donor, the more we can generate the growth and retention we need.

Guess what? Automation makes it easier to generate personalized interactions. And by "easier" we mean "more efficient."

Consider the data from Analytical Ones. It shows that the LTV of an average donor drops the longer you wait to ask for a second donation.

Data like these offer the most compelling case for incorporating automation, especially for organizations that have large donor databases. Without automation, you have to rely on a human to pull a report and send a handwritten welcome email or make a phone call or write a note. And then you have to rely on that same person to pull another report a month later and send a handwritten email asking for a second donation.

What happens when they miss someone? How do you ensure that they don't? There's a direct connection to lower revenue every time someone gets missed.

And from a personalization point of view, the human-generated email is nearly identical to an automated one. That's because a human creates a template for these welcome emails and then manually updates the fields just before hitting send. They will pull a report on a schedule and follow a set schedule for the drip. Automation does what people are already doing, but faster, and on a reliable cadence. And that's just email. Automation also supports a wide variety of fundraising communication media.

The goal of automation is to make the human fundraisers do their work better and more efficiently, all the while creating a more engaged donor base. For example, instead of having your staff spend their time manually pulling reports and clicking send over and over again, automation frees them up to do more in-person visits, phone calls, and more human interactions generally. Meanwhile, you can rely on the fact that all the necessary communications are going out in the background. In this sense, automation makes $1 + 1 = 3$.

Chapter 3:

The Values and Characteristics of a Responsive Nonprofit

Although nonprofits are all working towards unique goals, there are some common traits that exists among most of them. A belief in the possibilities of the future, for example, is something you'll find in nonprofits and the individuals that make up the organization. While most nonprofit characteristics are general, there are 5 that are specific to responsive nonprofits.

Responsive nonprofits focus on the future. They understand that the ways donors want to connect to their favorite organizations is much different than it was just a few years ago. So these organizations have started to re-prioritize certain behaviors and characteristics. If you're wondering whether your organization could make the switch to becoming more responsive to your constituents, consider these 5 essential nonprofit characteristics.

Empathetic

The foundation for responsive nonprofits is listening. In order to meet the needs of your modern donors, you have to know what they are. The only way to find out what they are is to listen when they tell you. But successful responsive nonprofits go beyond hearing their donors. They also empathize with their donors so that they can make meaningful connections.

Think about email marketing, for example. Nonprofits that don't prioritize empathy might see low open rates from a donor and assume they are just a lapsed donor who doesn't want to give anymore. However, a responsive nonprofit with an empathetic understanding of their donors might look for more nuanced clues. Perhaps after digging deeper, they'll discover that this donor cares most deeply about education programs and the last 7 emails they received focused on disease control. Of course they won't respond. But it takes empathy and intentional reporting to figure that out.

Empathetic understanding of your donors might take more time, but it also leads to more efficient engagements. It's much easier to make targeted campaigns that convert when you know exactly how your audience is feeling and why.

Collaborative

Responsive nonprofits are also collaborative. The nature of a relationship, whether it is personal or between donors and nonprofits, is to ebb and flow. Sometimes you'll need to lead the conversation and the next best action. Other times, you should let your donors lead. When other nonprofits might assume they always know the right thing to say, responsive nonprofits check in with their donors to confirm that the conversation is still interesting and helpful.

But don't stop at donor relationships when you direct your team to be more collaborative. Make a point to encourage collaboration between departments as well. For example, major donor representatives know exactly how to develop a donor relationship into a long-term, committed relationship. They've been cultivating those connections for years. Your marketing team, on the other hand, might need tips for what signs to look for or what information is essential for getting to know your donors motivations. Advocate for brainstorming and collaboration sessions between both departments so that every donor can receive a more comprehensive experience of your nonprofit.

Relational

Responsive nonprofits also see their donors not as people who provide the money, but as teammates helping the cause. The connection that responsive nonprofit teams create with their donors more closely resembles colleagues than anything else. Both sides are doing whatever they can to make the other successful. Both sides want to understand the other's goals and talents so that they can bring the best out of each other. It's a relational connection, not a transactional one.

The best way to prove that to your donors is to remain agile. Don't approach a conversation with rigid goals or outcomes that can only go one of two ways. Instead, create conversations that are open-ended. Reach out with questions about what the donors are interested in, what they've been thinking about lately and the last time they were excited about a milestone. Use their answers to suggest a next best action that will resonate.

Think about the variety of people in your life that add different things. For example, your mom is a nurturer when you need help. Your best friend is there to commiserate with you. Your boss helps mentor you with the next best move. You don't ask each of them the same question.

Instead, you modify your issue to fit the relationship you have with each one. The same logic applies to donors in a responsive fundraising framework.

Attentive

Responsive nonprofits always have a finger on the donors' pulse. They are paying attention to their donors' most important behaviors, both in the moment and over time. To responsive nonprofits, it's not enough just to reach a fundraising goal. They also want to know that they've built a deeper connection with their existing donors and set themselves up to create connections with new ones. Organizations can only achieve that level of connection if they are paying attention to the details.

A small warning on the note: make sure you trust the process. We've mentioned before that responsive nonprofits aren't afraid of taking calculated risks. Sometimes that means that you won't see big engagement numbers as soon as you become attentive. Don't give up on a smart campaign right away. Give it time to evolve. If, at the end, it didn't work, make the necessary adjustments. Just make sure that you're not paying such close attention that you lose sight of the goal.

Curious

Finally, and most importantly, responsive nonprofits are curious. They always want to know more. If you want your organization to be a successful responsive nonprofit, you must ask questions for breadth and depth. Remember that you are working towards a long-term relationship with each donor. You don't need to know everything right away. You want to continue to learn more with each interaction.

An easy way to instill a culture of curiosity in your organization is to encourage experimentation and be supportive in failure. If your team is too afraid to try something new, they will never learn new information about your donors. Keep everyone curious by saying yes to as many experiments, tests and ideas as possible. Obviously, it's important to set boundaries so that you're spending your money and resources wisely. But it's also important to confirm that curiosity is a good thing and failure is fine as long as it teaches you something.

To help make the small changes that will help you execute responsive fundraising, we've created a list of the top five values of responsive nonprofits. Add these to your current list of values, make some modifications to fit your specific goals or use them to start a conversation with stakeholders about where your nonprofit wants to go in the future.

No matter how you use these values, the result that matters is growing your organization so that you can do more good.

Generosity Is Deeply Personal

Responsive nonprofits understand that generosity is a deeply personal act. Donors aren't giving as an afterthought. More often, it's a response to a personal event in their life that moved them in a profound way. Responsive nonprofits don't take that vulnerability for granted.

In order to gain the trust of donors, your engagements should prove that you appreciate both their generosity and the events that lead them to give. Be curious about what led them to your organization and why they chose you over every other option. Listen to their personal stories and respond in a genuine way. Give them resources that speak directly to the things they've shared.

Most importantly, never ignore them when they reach out. Being ignored feels like rejection. Rejection pushes donors away from your organization and towards those that prioritize connection. Make sure your nonprofit is proving that you value connection at every opportunity.

All Givers Are Directly Connected to The Good

Responsive nonprofits understand that their role is to connect donors to the impact. Without repeated generosity from donors, nonprofits around the world would fail.

As such, all the fundraising celebrations, progress announcements and beneficiary impact statements need to be centered around the generosity of your donors. It's not the work that the nonprofit was able to do, but the generosity from donors that made it all possible.

You and your colleagues probably already feel this way, but make sure that it's obvious in the communications you send to donors. Check everything from your social media to your website and email campaigns for donor-centric language.

Any content that comes from your organization that doesn't directly tie your donors to the positive impact needs to be changed as soon as possible.

Donors Have More than Money to Give

Everyone goes through different seasons of their lives. Priorities shift and resources change. It happens all the time, but it's particularly obvious in donor behavior.

Sometimes the most meaningful contribution a donor can make is to give money. Other times, in order to feel helpful, donors might need to take action instead. Maybe there will be times when the best a person can do is stay up to date with the progress you're making in a particular program. Responsive nonprofits welcome all of it.

To be responsive, you have to value generosity completely. A donor who only gives money once a year but volunteers every other week still needs to be appreciated and engaged with.

Responsive nonprofits know this and execute campaigns that account for all the ways a person can give. They are thoughtful about suggestions they make and their timing. And they continually look for signals that their donors are ready to do something different to help impact the world in a positive way.

Staying open to possibilities and opportunities with your donors is how to build trust and grow your nonprofit in a meaningful way.

Good Is Done Together, Not Individually

This value speaks to donor relationships and internal ones. Responsive nonprofits are collaborative in all ways because they know the result is better.

In donor relationships, that means encouraging peer-to-peer campaigns, activating your network to get involved in creative ways that serve their interests and listening to ideas from your constituents.

Internally, that means freely sharing information, insights and ideas across departments. To be able to identify what motivations will inspire action, your organization needs to think about the big picture. Each team needs to work towards a single goal and help each department out however they can.

Remember, the goal for every campaign, initiative and communication is to move one step closer to completing the mission of your nonprofit. You can only do that if it is together.

Responsive Nonprofits Give More Than They Ask For

Finally, responsive nonprofits know that generosity begets generosity. This is the value that is most common in all nonprofits, but it doesn't always translate into donor relationships and other outward-facing communications.

Responsive nonprofits know that it is their responsibility to model the generosity they are asking for from donors. They are free with their gratitude, generosity and information. And it works.

Donors feel trust and commitment towards generous responsive nonprofits. By doing whatever it takes to foster that trust and commitment, responsive nonprofits are securing their place in donors' lives for many years to come.

Section 2:
28 Responsive Fundraising Plays

Now that you understand The Responsive Framework and the new expectations from modern donors, let's talk about how to execute responsive fundraising.

Try these 28 responsive fundraising plays to start improving your donor relationships and increasing generosity.

We've categorized them into Listen, Connect and Suggest, but feel free to get creative based on what you know about your donors. The more you try, the better you'll be at finding the right way to connect with all of your donors.

Chapter 4:

Responsive Fundraising Plays to Listen with Intention

How do you know what donors care about most? You listen.

Listening is the first part of The Responsive Framework, and it informs everything that follows. Before you can connect in a relevant way or suggest meaningful actions, you have to find out what your donors are interested in.

Play 1 : Talk Less, Listen More in Email

The fundamental shift to responsive fundraising, where the donor is at the center of all efforts, means your organization must resist the urge to tell donors what you think they should care about. Instead, seek out opportunities to hear from them.

New people engage with your nonprofit all the time, through events, email forms, social media, your website, peer recommendations, and even snail mail. You must be ready for them 24/7/365, and with responsive technology, you can be.

Establish two-way communication from the very beginning of the donor relationship. A three-part automated email series for new donors can help prioritize listening from your first conversations with the donor.

• **Email 1**: The first email welcomes the donor, sets up expectations, and asks about their preferences and interests. Allow your donors to tell you WHY they are passionate about your cause. Make sure the email is coming from a person (not "info@mynonprofit.org") and encourages real responses. You can collect the answers via a survey or other form, but it's also important to encourage donors to reply directly to your email. This gives them the freedom to give the full context of their why, plus it immediately signals that they are connected to real people at your organization.

- **Email 2**: The second email acknowledges the inputs from the first email, and suggests a series of potential next steps with the cause (education, telling friends, etc.). It also offers the opportunity to chat with a staff person about how they can maximize their impact apart from just giving. Make sure that this email is sent in a timely manner — don't make donors wait a week to hear back from your team. Marketing automation tools make it easy to respond immediately.

- **Email 3**: The third email showcases the impact of your work and celebrates the donor's involvement, while still inviting a response to the email or encouraging a 1-on-1 call to talk about the work. Ensure that the impact directly aligns with the programs or causes they care most about. Remember, the modern donor doesn't want to know what you think they should care about. They want you to respond to the things that matter most to them.

By opening up a line of two-way communication with your first emails you:
Signal that you are donor-centric and you value your donors as people.

Learn what motivates your donors to give quicker and more efficiently.

Create opportunities for donors to give more time, talent and social capital based on their individual interests

Play 2 : Tune Into Donor Signals

Everything a donor does and says about you is a signal. No single signal should inform your entire strategy, but together, the signals enable you to better understand each donor's intent. The result is personal connections that inspire loyalty and generosity.

There are many ways to listen to your donors, and each adds an important layer of context that can help your team create more effective responsive fundraising strategies.

Use the following digital listening techniques to help build a holistic, actionable view of each person in your database.

• Use lead forms on your website to gate downloadable assets. Include optional questions on the form to learn more about why each person is interested in your cause. Use tracking pixels to pre-fill form fields whenever possible to make the experience convenient for your donors, thus giving them time to answer your more involved questions.

- Use digital behaviors, like website visits, email clicks or online donations to gauge the engagement level and interests of each person. Good tracking tools (email platforms and web tracking pixels) allow you to attach activity to each donor, automatically tag donors based on the CTA or topic they engage with, and then automate follow up based on their activity.

- Ensure that you're listening to the engagement behavior on each follow-up communication, as well, to maintain relevancy and connection to your donors.

- Social listening provides a mechanism to track your donor's interest via their social profiles. Following your donors on social or automatically scraping their social feeds (more here later) gives you the ability to find out who your donors are and what they care about without asking them to take any extra steps.

The value of collecting all these different signals simultaneously is to create a more comprehensive donor profile. With more information, you have the opportunity to nuance and personalize each engagement so that, over time, your fundraising is more relevant and effective.

Play 3 : Quarterly Surveys and Interviews

Responsive nonprofits regularly get formal feedback from their donors in the form of surveys and donor interviews. These engagements ensure that you are in tune with the passions of your donors and can deeply understand the reasons behind their commitment to your cause.

The result is an ability to refine your fundraising strategy AND provide significant proof to donors that they have real input in your cause.

Use quarterly surveys to determine what issues/ solutions motivate your donors. Always push yourself and your organization to go further with your questions. Ask about whether your programs resonate with donors regarding each issue.

Don't shy away from the less-than-ideal answers, because all data inputs will help you be a better responsive fundraiser. Here's how to start:

- Create two segments: donors who've given in the last 12 months and those that have given in the last 36 months but not the last 12. Every four months you'll rotate the list and send the survey to one third of each segment. This ensures you're seeking feedback from each individual on an annual basis through this method.

- Now, create a simple survey that asks the following questions:

  - On a scale of 0-10, how likely are you to recommend Organization to a friend or family member?

  - Why did you give the score above?

  - What could we do to improve your experience as a key supporter of Organization?

  - What sparked you to give to Organization?

  - For current donors: Why do you continue to give?

  - For inactive donors: Why did you stop giving in the last year?

- Then, put together a two email series that you'll use to invite the targeted donors to complete the survey. Make sure that you're using language and messaging that appeals to the donor segment and their specific interest. In our world of busy inboxes, relevant subject lines and valuable information is the key to conversions.

- Make sure to create an email that is sent to anyone who completes your survey. Thank them for their input, reiterate why you're asking and what you'll do with the feedback, and set expectations on what they should expect now (i.e. a summary of your findings and what the org will do differently now). Ideally, you'd set this up to be sent out automatically after the donor gave their input.

- Be sure to have a follow-up plan. If a donor shares a low likelihood to recommend, you should have a follow-up plan, or if a donor praises your org, plan for how you will thank them for their support and suggest they get more deeply involved.

Remember, the longer it takes for you to follow up on your donors' generosity (including survey answers), the more likely it is that they will lose trust in your organization. The two-way relationship means that you need to be as engaged as they are.

Play 4 : Supplement with Third-Party Wealth, Demographic and Social Data

It can be difficult to collect all the donor data that you'll need to connect more deeply with each person. After you've surveyed donors, watched their web behavior, and analyzed their giving history, there will likely still be a few data points that you'd like to know.

Thankfully, there is an abundance of public data available about your donors. Social media profiles, real estate data, corporate filings, public giving data and other online data sources can all combine to give you a rich profile of each person in your database. If you're just starting with outside data sources we'd recommend integrating your CRM with the following:

• Wealth data through vendors like DonorSearch help provide insights into the financial capacity of each donor. Wealth data can provide Charitable Giving Activity, Real Estate Holdings, Political Giving, Business Affiliations, Stock Ownership and more. Wealth data should update in your CRM automatically when in a contact is entered. Once appended, it can be used to automatically segment donors, notify team members, or prioritized outreach.

- Similarly, social media scraping can be used to pull public data from social media platforms and other profile-based web sites into your CRM. Good social scraping uses your donor's email or home address to collect behavior and preference-based data from thousands of social media sites.

Data should be automatically entered into your CRM in real time, so that you always have the most accurate picture of each individual. This appended data should include images of the donor, links to their social profiles, employment and age information, etc. Social data can be used to fill out donor profiles, identify influencers in your database, or determine the interests and preferences of each donor.

Assign individuals on your team to regularly assess the data included in your donor profiles, like you would with survey results. The more time you dedicate to listening to each signal available to you, the easier it will be to create fundraising campaigns that work.

Play 5 : Pay Attention To Social Media

As a responsive nonprofit, you need to seek out channels that give you access to your current donors and any potential donors. Largely, that means a presence on social media that extends beyond an information distribution channel or a place to loudly promote new fundraising campaigns. Instead, use your organization's profiles to listen to the conversations around your cause, your donors, your organization, and the general sentiment towards generosity. Here are a few strategies to improve your social listening.

- Identify which of your donors are active on social media. Who has a large audience? Do you have any donors that actively participate in a prominent influencer's content? Once you know these details, you can use marketing automation to promote advocacy opportunities to these donors.

- Browse LinkedIn to identify good prospects in your donor base for business partnerships or matching gift opportunities.

- Follow your organization's hashtag or the conversation around your current fundraising campaigns. Who is most active in those exchanges? What can their conversations tell you about their passions or preferences?

- Ask questions on social media with at least one third of your posts. Who responds? What do they care about?

- Show up in Quora groups, discussions boards, or LinkedIn groups associated with your broad cause. Just listen and participate without promoting your nonprofit. What do people care about? What change do they want to see in the world?

Once you've listened, make sure to log what you've learned in your CRM and use your findings to refine your overall messaging. When more of your team members can access a wealth of information on each donor, you give yourself better opportunities to come up with the big ideas that leave a lasting impression on your donors.

Play 6 : Map Relationships

Your donors don't exist in a bubble. They are members of communities, faith organizations, clubs, and schools. We know from previous generations, that community-driven generosity is one of the more powerful forces in fundraising.

When you consider these location-based relationships, you can give donors more personal suggestions and help build micro-movements for your cause. Here's how to get started with relationship mapping based on geography.

• Display all of your donors on a Google map using home and/or work addresses you have in their donor profile.

• Search for dense pockets of donors within a neighborhood or zip code.

• Look for commonalities between donors who make up those pockets. Be sure to prioritize commonalities that are based in motivations and values, rather than demographic data like age or occupation. See if you can find a local chapter of your cause, local faith congregation involvement, or local influencer who is connected with all donors.

• Reach out to the committed influencers and see if they'd be willing to host a donor impact event in their community. Be sure that your initial outreach is highly personalized, based on the information you know. Highlight what the impact event can add to their own values, not what it can do for your nonprofit. Stay donor-centric in all communications.

This approach helps solidify your base of support in an area and capitalize on existing geo-graphic momentum. Remember, giving is dramatically influenced by peers and local community. Capitalizing on existing relationships adds social proof and community to your donor cultivation strategy.

Play 7 : Ask Questions in Unexpected Places

Never miss an opportunity to ask your donors a question. Stay curious and encourage all your team members to remain so as well. From casual conversations at events to formal surveys, every communication is a chance to learn more about your donors.

- Evaluate the donor experience after they make a gift. What are you doing in that moment to advance your donor relationships? Use the online thank you page along with paper receipts to learn more. Include a short survey asking why the person gave and what they'd like to see in the future from your organization.

- Send follow-up communications to everyone who answers the surveys that acknowledges their answers and sets expectations for how you'll use them, and in what timeline, and provide a new suggestion for getting more involved in your organization.

- Use the Net Promoter Score (NPS) question on receipts and confirmation emails to see how satisfied donors are with your organization. An NPS survey simply asks users to rate the question "How likely are you to recommend us to a friend?" on a scale of 1-10. It provides donors the opportunity to tell you about concerns so that you can try to remedy those issues before losing that donor for good. Report on NPS questions every 9 to 12 months to measure donor experience, pick up additional signals and learn about ways you can improve.

- Segment donors who give you a score of 9 or 10 on the NPS questions to enroll them in a donor advocacy engagement sequence. Provide relevant information and opportunities they can sign up for to be more directly involved in your work and programs.

- Ask donors who haven't given in 18 months or more for honest feedback about what changed and what you could have done better. Many times, lapsed donors don't feel heard or recognized. Listening to donors honest feedback might help re-acquire the donor but, more importantly, you can use what you learn to improve donor retention and engagement in the future.

Play 8 : Evaluate Your Feedback System

As Nicholas Ellinger pointed out in *The New Nonprofit*, good feedback systems:

- Are systems. They help you create a process for collecting, reviewing, and implementing feedback. Don't ask people for information you cannot implement into a plan with action items.

- Are simple and standardized. You're looking for easy and repeatable here. Remember, responsive fundraising is all about scaling your efforts to include more donors. If it is too complicated or dependent on nuanced information, you will likely abandon it for past habits.

- Give donors a reason to participate. Tell them why you're asking, using "because" phrases, as in "We're asking for your opinion, because we want you to be happy."

- Allow the user to pick the channel. Give people options for how they respond. Do they want to talk to a real-live human, or would they rather fill out a form online? Do they want to be anonymous? Encourage participation by accommodating a range of preference.

- Have follow-up. It doesn't feel great to give an opinion or answer a question and never hear back. In fact, to donors, it can feel like another way nonprofits are taking advantage of their generosity. Let people know you're listening by updating them on any changes you've made or consensus you've reached, responding to their specific concerns or questions, and even just thanking them for participating.

• Do your current feedback systems include these attributes? Find ways to refine your feedback system to close the loop on donor feedback.

Play 9 : Seek Donor Preferences & Group Donors by Persona

All the inputs you listen for will start to reveal common themes among your donors. Your survey data, social listening, behavior tracking, and communication indexing will work together to show you who your donors are and what they care most about.

Soon, you'll be able to craft your unique donor personas, which can help you improve marketing automation, donor relationships and fundraising.

For example, an animal charity may have bird and cat people, or vegans and life-long pet owners. They may have a mix of Democrats and Republicans. Colleges have alumni, faculty, parents, and distant fans. Aid groups may have a combination of disaster relief people and regional advocates. Each group's preferences should inform their messaging and communications.

Here's how to create your donor personas:

• Once you have collected enough data (both over time and across your donor base), build a donor persona for each group. Include motivational data, engagement data, preferences, demographic information, and any other specific pieces of information that helps you get to know each segment.

• Use each donor persona to curate specific content and communications strategies that are highly personalized and relevant for that donor persona.

• Use targeted stories and statistics in direct mail appeals based on the persona of the person getting the letter. Make sure that you include messaging that you've verified will resonate with each person based on the persona they match most closely with.

• Create landing pages on your website with content specifically targeted for each persona. Use Search Engine Optimization strategies to show up in searches by prospects who fit the criteria for that persona and are looking for new causes to support.

• Create email and web content based on topics that are most relevant to your donor personas. Identify which medium each persona prefers so that you can get the most return from each piece of content. Personalize your promotion of each video, blog, ebook, etc., based on donor personas so each person receives the best experience possible.

Responsive nonprofits use the data they have in order to make the most impact with each engagement. Donor personas are a critical step to ensuring that your donors convert on each action you suggest to them.

Chapter 5:

Plays to Help You Connect in Relevant Ways

Connection is all about effective, relevant communication with each donor. It includes activities traditionally known as cultivation and stewardship.

By applying what you've learned about your donors from your listen plays, you can create connections that educate, engage and inspire your donors. Often, connection is where donors receive the most value as a supporter of your nonprofit.

For modern nonprofits, personal connection isn't just for your major donors. New technologies like marketing automation, predictive data analytics and web/social listening tools make it possible to personally connect with all donors.

These Connect plays will help you implement tactics that connect personally with all your donors and put your donors at the center of your fundraising.

Play 10 : Keep Your Communication Human

Nonprofits know that people can't form lasting connections with generic communications. But, without marketing automation, it's nearly impossible to scale personalized, genuine connections with each individual donor. Responsive nonprofits operate in the sweet spot between automation and one-to-one communication.

You can build the human connection with your donors by adding warm, personalized elements to all your communications. Our friends at NextAfter have conducted many nonprofit email experiments, and they recommend humanizing your fundraising emails by:

• Sending your next fundraising email from a real person's name, not a generic organization email address, like "info@organization.org." People are more likely to open something from a person instead of a faceless organization.

• Not focusing on the length of the message. Instead, write as much or as little as you need to convey what the need is, what the solution is, why a supporter must act to make it happen and what happens if they don't.

- Only using images if they will strengthen the value of your appeal.

- Skipping your organization's standard email template for anything outside of your monthly newsletter. Send a plain text email like you'd send a friend whenever possible.

- Writing with a conversational tone and voice. Aim to sound like a real human being instead of a formal organization. Your email should feel like one person writing to one other person, not a mass message. Try writing a first draft using speech-to-text on your phone, or reading aloud your draft and correcting it to sound more natural.

Personalized communications like this will make it easier for your donors to trust that you care about them and what they care about. Trust is ultimately what leads to increased generosity.

Play 11 : Earn Trust, Don't Rent or Steal Attention

Renting a list of contacts in order to send an acquisition mailing focused solely on your organization's financial needs isn't an effective way to connect with today's donor.

Organizations who rely on bombarding cold names with "me"-focused institutional messages aren't building authentic relationships, they're renting space in donors' mailboxes. Donors didn't decide to be on those lists and they don't yet trust the organization sending them.

In today's hyper-connected world, we are exposed to thousands of marketing messages a day. No one can possibly consume that much information in 24 hours. So, we ignore any message that comes from an organization we don't know, trust, or have a personal connection to.

Today, donors have all the power. They turn to their friends, like-purposed community members, and peer reviews to find causes to support. They want to connect on their own terms, and rarely are those terms, "I'll support whoever bought access to my address."

Instead of randomly showing up in a donor's mailbox, organizations need to earn trust by giving donors something of value. "Value" doesn't mean tote bags or branded magnets. It's about providing donors with meaning in a way that is relevant to them. Create value through your content, and donors will become more connected to your work and your story.

If your strategy does include buying list for acquisition, focus on how you are providing real value to your prospects. Make your offer about *them* not *you*. Remember, generosity begets generosity.

Try these tactics to make each direct mail piece more effective to purchased lists:

• Audit the list before you send mailers. Do what you can to make connections between their information and your current donor list. Can you alter the messaging to be location-based? Is there value in making connections to a local social influencer? Any information you can include to make the message less generic will grab the attention of new contacts.

• Test the times that you send your direct mail pieces to purchased lists. Try to discover whether you make better connections with new contacts during seasons that aren't focused around giving. For example, don't try to create a relationship and ask for a financial gift during November and December when mailboxes are flooded. Instead, try fostering that relationship in the beginning of the year.

• Include a variety of calls-to-action on your direct mailers. Create a testing structure that reveals what new contacts are most likely to do upon receiving their first mail piece from you. Will they watch a video? Sign up for your newsletter? Follow you on social media? Give a gift? You'll see a much better return on your mail strategy if you find the right CTAs.

• Let unresponsive contacts go. Don't continue to send information to contacts who aren't responding to your efforts. Use your resources to cultivate relationships and optimize your current strategies to improve your return. Not all donors will want to support your cause, and that is totally fine! That means you can spend more time with the people who do.

Take a look at the growth the Cornell Lab of Ornithology has experienced via targeted content marketing to understand the value of earning trust rather than stealing attention. Using responsive techniques and valuable content, they were able to build a connected community of birders.

Media Cause writes:

"Year after year, the Lab has been able to increase online fundraising numbers by growing their email list and inspiring current supporters to give. The Lab has a wealth of great content that inspires a shared love of birds and highlights the critical importance of bird conservation."

Birders come for the bird content, but stay and become donors once they learn more about the Lab. Using content marketing, the Lab has grown its annual revenue from $400,000 in 2012 to nearly $4M in 2019.

Play 12 : Stand For Something with a Clear Unique Value Proposition

The modern world is divided, nuanced, and complicated. In the midst of all that gray area, we're drawn to those who are clear about what they stand for and what they're against.

Responsive nonprofits communicate what they're for, and seek to inspire, activate, and rally like-purposed people together. Through content, stories, events, and campaigns, they connect with a community who shares their goals.

Show what you stand for with deliberate storytelling that showcases your cause, your heroes and villains. Consider the Instagram video from Preemptive Love, in which they discuss the deaths of people, particularly children, seeking asylum.

Preemptive Love takes a bold stand — they "exist to end war." In this post, they identify the love of power as the villain that needs to be overcome, more than any one political entity. They're not wishy-washy, and you don't have to wonder about what their values are. Donors know exactly what they're supporting.

In one sentence:

• Write out the *unique* value that your nonprofit creates that isn't accomplished by any other organization.

• Write out what the ramifications are to the world if your mission is not accomplished.

- Modify that sentence to speak to the different goals of your donor personas. Make sure that each persona can feel connected and aligned to the mission you're working towards.

- Use that sentence as often as possible to remind your donor base exactly what they're giving to and why your organization is be option for accomplishing that goal.

Deepen your donor relationships by including your donors in the conversations around your mission statement. As you grow and the focus of your organization evolves, your statement might require updating. Let the donors be part of that process. After all, they are at the center of everything you do and every possibility you have for the future.

Play 13 : Automate Welcome Series and New Donor On-boarding

Donor churn may be the biggest single problem facing most nonprofits. On average, 76% of donors will never give again after their first gift. Reducing your first gift churn by even 10% can have a massive impact on the long-term value of your donors.

The most proven and predictable way to reduce new donor churn is with a New Donor Welcome Series. The goal of this series is to onboard new donors by educating them and providing value before you ask for the next gift.

With marketing automation, you can determine the frequency, timeline and content included in the New Donor Welcome Series for each individual. The following marketing automation sequence is a great start for organizations who don't yet have a Welcome sequence.

Day 0 – Email 1

Theme: Welcome and thank you!

Content: Thank you photo of team. More about the problem you're helping us solve in a unique way... What interests you about the cause?

CTA: Tell Us More!

Day 1 – Email 2

Theme: Introducing our community

Content: Nonprofit impact video and stories about unique ways people like you are making a difference. Thank them again for their impact.

CTA: See More Impact Stories

Day 3 – Thank You Call

Theme: Gratitude and curiosity.

Content: Thank you for your gift! More about the impact you're having. What made you give? How can we serve you?

CTA: None.

Day 5 – Email 3

Theme: Ways to help.

Content: Volunteer opportunities, advocacy opportunities, program information, and link to social feeds

CTA: Follow Us on Social.

Day 15 – Email 4

Theme: Learn more

Content: Infographic about the cause

CTA: Complete Our Quiz!

Day 18 – Welcome Packet in the Mail

Theme: Giving

Content: Re-establish value through a story of impact. Refer to some of the stories and stats you've sent through email, thank them again. Appeal for a donation

CTA: Make a Donation (if initial gift was under $100 ask for a recurring gift)

Note: For gifts over a certain threshold it makes sense to assign a handwritten thank you note to a team member as well.

Day 21 – Email 6

Theme: Giving

Content: Re-establish value through a story of impact. Appeal for a donation.

CTA: Make a Donation (if initial gift was under $100 ask for a recurring gift)

After each person has completed the email welcome series, add them to your newsletter list and any other lists that are targeted to the interests they expressed during the welcome series.

Play 14 : Use Predictive Data to Automate Influencer Outreach

Your influencers are the megaphone for your cause. In the new landscape of fundraising peers, influencers can drive far more successful new donor acquisition campaigns than traditional models.

It's critical that you identify your influencers quickly and segment them for specific communication. You can identify influencers by listening for:

• Number of known relationships in your existing database. Are they already connected with other key donors or partners?

• Number of Twitter followers. Are they a social influencer or do they have a large social voice?

• Geographic density. Are there a lot of key donors or prospects in their neighborhood or nearby?

• Peer-to-Peer activity. Have they previously run P2P campaigns on behalf of your organization?

• Corporate or Philanthropic Activity. Did social scraping or their LinkedIn profile reveal corporate influence, board membership, political influence, etc?

Automatically tag influencers based on the criteria that you've set for your Influencer persona.

Set a marketing automation workflow that includes:

- 2-3 emails that describe the impact similar influencers are having on the cause. Provide specific examples of work done by other influencers. Whenever possible, make the connection between the topics you know they care about and the campaign you are suggesting they run.

  The more relevant your appeals, the more likely they are to be successful. Spend the extra time doing research to ensure that they don't feel like you're sending a generic sequence without genuine interest in their values and audience.

- Create an "Ambassador" or "Advocacy" club, and then invite the influencer to join using an online form at no cost. This provides a feeling of "insider" belonging to your influencers.

  Use an automation workflow to provide participants with materials they need to understand your cause and how to talk about it in a way that will resonate with their audience. Arm them with the necessary tools to run a successful campaign immediately so you can capitalize on the moments they are most excited about the opportunity.

- Follow up with a phone call to brainstorm with the influencer about ways they might want to get involved. Understand that you are the expert on your cause, but they are the expert on their audience. Make sure to prepare for the phone call, but stay responsive to their interests and needs.

Influencers should be treated the same way the rest of your donors are treated. Make sure their interests and goals are at the center of your partnership to ensure a lasting relationship and better fundraising.

Play 15 : Automate Lapse and Pre-Lapse Sequences to Reduce Churn

Like first time donor churn, lapsed core donors can have a tremendously negative impact on nonprofits. Without a deep, personal connection to your nonprofit, they can easily forget why your cause was important to them in the first place. The business of life and work replace their focus and they don't prioritize giving to you.

To help prevent lapsing it's critical to quickly identify lapsed and pre-lapsed donors. Each group needs a re-engagement strategy to remind donors about the impact they are making in the world and what your organization is doing to meet their goals and live their values. Here's a standard marketing automation workflow that can be impactful in reducing churn.

Day 0 – Email 1

> **Theme**: Thank you for your impact!

> **Content**: We've noticed you haven't given recently. More about the problem you're helping us solve in a unique way. Do you have questions or concerns we can help with?

> **CTA**: Ask a Question or Give Us a Call

74

Day 3 – Thank You Call

Theme: Gratitude and curiosity

Content: Thank you for giving in the past. More about the impact you're having. What made you give? Is there something we can do differently?

CTA: Give Us Your Thoughts.

Day 5 – Email 3

Theme: Stories of Impact

Content: We miss you! Re-establish value through a story of impact. Infographic about the cause.

CTA: Share Your Impact with Friends.

Day 10 – Lapsed Direct Mail Letter

Theme: Giving

Content: We miss you! Re-establish value through a story of impact. Refer to some of the stories and stats you've sent through email. Appeal for a donation

CTA: Make a Donation

Note: When possible also send a handwritten card of gratitude.

As with all of your marketing automation workflows, keep an eye on performance metrics. It is critical that you provide enough value to lapsed and pre-lapsed donors before you ask for another gift.

If you ask too soon, you risk losing donors forever. Use the engagement metrics to optimize your workflow based on donor personas for an even better return.

Play 16 : Automate Donor - Milestone Acknowledgments

Donors want to feel like an important member of your organization. They want to feel appreciated for their contribution. One of the easiest ways to express gratitude is by thanking donors in a special way when they hit particular giving milestones.

This type of milestone recognition varies for each organization but here's a sample automation workflow that we've found helpful.

Automation ensures that every donor is recognized in a timely manner without requiring your team to do any additional work. This workflow should automatically run in the background and kick off when key milestones are hit.

$1,000 in total donations:

- **Day 1**: Assign Task to Development Rep for follow-up thank you call

- **Day 1**: Add a Tag for "Mid-Level" Donor

- **Day 1**: Send "Life-to-Date Giving $1,000" Thank You Email

- **Day 3**: Assign task to Director of Development for Thank You Handwritten Note

- **Day 3:** Follow donor in CRM or assign to a mid-level donor portfolio

Of course, creating milestone celebrations for small donors is important as well. Donors who are recognized frequently tend to have higher average value because they remain loyal for longer. Adjust the recognition and workflows based on the level of commitment from each donor.

Play 17 : Lead with Stories, Follow on with Stats

Humans are motivated by stories, not numbers. Stories that focus on one person inspire more giving than statistics because humans evoke empathy and a desire to help. Without a central character to identify with, people have a hard time understanding the problem or relating to those affected. Thus, it's easier to move on without taking action.

Numbers may give a quick overview of the issue, but stories are what make us care. Stories connect us to other people and inspire giving.

Look for opportunities to tell stories to your supporters that highlight the humans behind the cause. Build a strong, direct connection between donors and beneficiaries as often as possible.

Use The Adventure Project as an example. They send monthly updates to "The Collective," their group of recurring gift contributors. Each month, they feature the story of a woman who benefited from the program the donors funded.

"The Collective" stays inspired and engaged by seeing the human impact their donations make, month after month. Instead of a vague sense of "helping women in the developing world," they have specific people in mind.

Even a semi-fictional character can resonate with audiences, like the YMCA of America's "Zoe for President" campaign. They created the character of Zoe, a one-year-old girl who would run for president in 2064.

The YMCA says, "The campaign highlights the potential the Y sees in all kids to grow up and change the world if they're nurtured properly and supported along the way. Through Y initiatives like childcare, academic enrichment, mentorship, college prep, job training, and more, kids have the opportunities to succeed, grow, and one day, maybe even become president."

Supporters could "donate to Zoe's campaign" by making a donation to the Y. The story engaged imaginations, and gave a specific character to focus on, rather than a generic "children are important," message.

To get started:

- Write out your three most compelling stories of impact. Focus on relatable stories that create real emotional connection.

- Be clear about the hero of each story (it's not your organization!)

- Be clear about the antagonist and urgent conflict in each story.

- Show how the donor can change the story by partnering with your organization.

- Find ways to tell each story in videos that are less than 2 minute.

- Supplement video with a CTA focused on your donors impact and a statistic that validates your impact.

- Parlay videos into social posts, blogs, event trailers, etc. Translate stories in short written vignettes for direct mail.

Chapter 6:

Plays to Suggest the Next Best Action

Responsive suggestions follow insights discovered by listening, provided via the right channels identified in Connect. Each suggestion are based on the relationship you have with the donor, not an arbitrary timetable set by the organization.

Donors are people, and no one likes being treated like an ATM. Too often, nonprofits only look to donors for donations, skipping all the unique ways they might want to contribute to your cause. If you look at donors solely through a transactional lens, you'll miss out on a range of contributions.

Play 18 : Variable Gift Arrays

One of the most frustrating experiences for donors is when they are asked for a financial gift that is dramatically disconnected from their previous giving or capacity. Common donor stories include:

"I just gave them $100,000 for the new building. Why the heck are they asking me for $50 a month?"

"I'm a college student who volunteers for that nonprofit 10 hours a week. Do they really think I have $10K to donate?"

Fortunately, modern data analytics can help you solve this problem by varying the gift ask and gift array for each donor based on capacity. You know your donors historical giving and you can grab their wealth capacity (see the Listen play for public data sources).

By combining this data you can ask for exactly the right amount at the right time. You can even use a "Suggested Gift Amount" generated by predictive data analytics to shift your suggested gift arrays to the range that's right for each donor. This approach can be applied to your online giving form using a tracking pixel or it can be used as a merge field in your direct mail pieces.

By tailoring the gift ask for each person in your database, you'll not only alienate fewer givers but you'll dramatically increase your response rate and average gift amount.

Play 19 : Ask For More Than Money

We know that today's donors want to be part of something bigger than themselves. They want to be more than just a checkbook. It only makes sense to offer them more ways to get involved.

When you learn about a donor's interests and observe their behavior, you may learn that the appropriate suggestion isn't money. Knowing when to provide value instead of ask for money builds loyalty and greater engagement from donors. It brings them close to your cause.

Realistically, you can only ask for money so many times before alienating donors. Suggesting non-monetary next steps is often more impactful for your organization and more gratifying for donors.

Ask for Time

Donations of time can include traditional volunteer opportunities, advocacy at local events, or peer-to-peer campaigning. It can also include visiting your nonprofit in person to get a better sense for your work and what you are accomplishing in the world. Use surveys and social media to find your donors' particular super powers and then suggest that they engage using their particular talents.

Ask for Influence

Your donors already live in networks and digital tribes. Rather than trying to build a tribe around your institution, ask donors to introduce you to their existing tribes. They can share their influence via peer-to-peer fundraising, social media posts, hosting events, inviting friends to volunteer, leveraging their businesses, or making strategic partnerships between your organization and their faith group or networks.

Pre-record a webinar with a few donors who've used their influence to further promote via fundraising, advocacy, or amplification. Then use social listening to determine which donors have larger social audiences.

Create a donor advocacy workflow that is a series of three emails that invite these social donors to watch the webinar where you unpack how they can use their influence to advocate for the cause.

The team at charity:water does a great job of leveraging corporate and celebrity influencers along with the superpowers of their supporters to increase impact. Check out some of their work for more ideas.

Ask for Expertise

Some donors may wish to lend their professional expertise and acumen, founding an advisory counsel or participating in meetups to give their advice on topics like marketing, real estate, finance, or legal matters. Some may prefer to lend expertise around their passions rather than their profession.

Don't be afraid to ask donors for help in their areas of expertise or passions. Keep in mind that donors will have varying availability, so you have to be prepared with a wide array of opportunities.

The best suggestions often include specific time constraints and objectives so that donors know exactly what they're signing up for and why they are the best person to help. That said, it's good to leave the door open to listen to donors and let them suggests the ways they think they might add value.

Play 20 : Mobilize Donors, Don't Manage Them

Traditional fundraising tries to push donors to do what the nonprofit wants them to do. Responsive fundraisers act as a pathway for like-purposed people to connect and give. The organization creates the environments and resources that equip supporters to be successful.

One nonprofit did this by empowering supporters to be "Advocates." They created an Advocate Facebook Group, and provided supporters with an Advocate kit that included stories, messages, cause-related statistics, facts about the nonprofit, and calls-to-action.

Hundreds of people joined to share their time and influence with the cause. Some had blogs and businesses, others were students and parents.

The nonprofit mobilized their community by distributing stories and videos for them to share, sparking conversations between members that lived locally, and celebrating supporters who organized their own fundraisers.

The nonprofit was a facilitator, the community did the fundraising. They had a tremendous sense of ownership of the cause, and a deep connection to the nonprofit. For an easy way to identify who to mobilize and how, try these strategies.

- Identify qualifications of donors who are most likely to enjoy advocating for your organization.

- Enroll them in an advocate recruitment engagement campaign to understand their level of excitement for participating in a program.

- Call each individual to understand specific goals, passions, and experience level.

- Connect like-purposed individuals via email. Describe their common goals and interests and suggest ways that they can make a direct impact on the work your nonprofit is doing.

- Host weekly online conferences to encourage advocates, check on progress, and provide new ideas to move their project forward.

- At the end of the project, follow up with questions about what they loved and what they wish was different. Use what they tell you to optimize the experience for new advocates.

Play 21: Automate Planned Giving Outreach Using Demographic/Wealth Data

Recent studies tell us that, over the next 30 years, Americans will see almost $68 trillion passed down from Baby Boomers. In many cases, these Boomers are looking to leave a lasting legacy with their wealth. As a nonprofit, it's important that you're educating Boomers on *how* planned giving works and *why* your organization can build their legacy in a unique way.

Data analytics can be a critical tool for connecting with these donors and suggesting the next step of a planned gift. Use this data and automation play to be helpful in increasing your planned giving portfolio

Automatically identify donors who:

• Have given for the last 3 years at least

• Are over 60

• **Optional**: Have a net worth of over $1M according to purchased wealth data

When a donor matches this criteria you can:

- Automatically send a letter and 2 emails with the sole purpose of educating them on planned giving. Tailor the messaging to what you know about their motivations, interests, and giving history.

- Assign a task to a member of your team to follow up via phone to answer any questions. The goal of the call is primarily education. Get comfortable with the fact that they may have a passion for other organizations. Encourage their generosity to ANY organization and talk about how your nonprofit might uniquely fit into their planning.

Play 22 : Amplify Other Voices

Have you ever met someone who exclusively talked about themselves? It doesn't take too long to tune out or start avoiding them, does it? It's the same for organizations. Your own messages about how great you are won't resonate with donors for long. It's much more interesting to hear praise from someone else.

Leverage social proof points to confirm to donors and potential donors that your organization is making an impact and doing great work. Testimonies and personal experience can mean a lot to supporters who are getting to know you, and people love to see that "people like them" are involved.

Conduct a simple survey of why people give, and ask:

• Why do you give to Organization?

• Would you recommend Organization to others?

• How can we improve?

Just like you identified donor groups based on interests, you'll find trends in your survey results. You may find that some people give because of direct experience with your cause, while others are motivated by civic responsibility, or seeing your work in the community. For each trend that emerges, choose a story from their responses. Add these stories to fundraising campaigns and your welcome series.

Highlight your donor community with a "Why Give?" landing page on your website that includes these donor stories, along with 10-20 quotes from your survey results. For example, World Help features a range of donors talking about why they give. It makes giving seem accessible.

Play 23 : Make Fundraising Everyone's Job

Donors make it possible for your nonprofit to operate. It's the reason you and your colleagues have jobs that you love. To that end, donor relationships are a priority for everyone in the organization, not just development professionals. Programs, operations, finance and administration are all equally impacted by donor activity.

"Creating a culture of fundraising" sounds complicated, but it's really about inviting everyone at your organization into the action. Start including them with:

• A one-hour, all-hands-on-deck monthly meeting where everyone comes together to write thank you notes to donors and volunteers, or make thank you calls

• An email to the whole organization that shares recent impact stories, donor testimonies, and a list of ways to amplify the latest fundraising efforts. This alone can give your program and other staff stories to share and ideas for engaging people they interact with.

- Inviting donors to visit your offices or facility monthly, if possible. Host an open house, or give an open invitation for donors to schedule a visit. This lets staff interact with donors and hear their personal stories, and vice versa.

- Create an internal dashboard that highlights key fundraising KPIs and share it broadly, so everyone knows exactly where your nonprofit is compared to goals, how many new donors have partnered with the org, and how many have stopped giving. This level of transparency can help push everyone to keep fundraising and donors top of mind.

Play 24 : Personal For All

Traditionally, marketers evaluate contacts with RFM (Recency, Frequency, Monetary Value). Responsive fundraisers still consider those elements, but go beyond it to include things like donor interests, enthusiasm, history, and feedback. They consider a broader context.

For instance, imagine you have a group of donors who are also volunteers. Each year, they take on a small peer-to-peer fundraising project. If you only look at RFM, you could conclude that you need to focus on getting these donors to give more frequently, or transition to larger gifts.

However, if you listened and connected with these donors, you'd find that they consider their volunteerism to be their most important contribution because they are unable to make larger financial gifts. The nonprofit constantly asking for more frequent donations is going to make them feel unappreciated and unseen. Would you blame them for becoming less involved?

What if, instead, you asked them to train other volunteers to do their own peer-to-peer campaigns? That would demonstrate that you value their expertise and service, help them connect with each other and the volunteers they train, and deepen their ties to the organization, while growing your fundraising.

Play 25: Multi-Channel, One Conversation

Marketing research has shown us that most people don't respond to the first "touch" of a message. They need to encounter it several times before taking action.

As such, you need to create an engagement strategy that allows your donors to see your organization across a variety of channels. You can use each of them to build one continuing conversation. Include email, direct mail, social media, your website, phone calls, events, and in-person interactions in your communications strategy and flows.

This doesn't mean you copy and paste your content everywhere and call it a day. You don't have to tell identical stories on each channel, but your suggestion should be the same.

If the suggestion is, "Become a recurring giver," then you may tell a story about a specific person served by your programs on social media, feature a Q & A video with a monthly giver on your website, and send an infographic about the impact of monthly giving via email. Each message is appropriate to its medium, but they all point to the same thing.

Play 26: Always Celebrate

People value milestones, recognition and celebration. From communal celebrations like national holidays to personal markers like a year of sobriety, the calendar provides many opportunities to mark an occasion.

Organizations have an opportunity to tap into our love of celebration, and personally connect and make celebratory suggestions. First, look for personal milestones, like:

- Donor anniversaries:"You've supported Organization for three years! Wow! Thank you! In that time, you've given $XXXX, providing programming for 300 students like Mandy. Watch her story here, and share it with anyone who needs a little inspiration. Happy anniversary!"

- 100 hours volunteered: Send an infographic about what 100 volunteering hours accomplishes, invite them to report back to you on their experience.

- $10,000 raised through peer-to-peer fundraising: Ask them to mentor a new fundraiser or give feedback on the campaign.

Collective milestones are another opportunity for celebratory suggestions. Reach out to celebrate with your community every time you hit a goal, like your 1,000th student graduation, opening a new facility, or 15th year in operation.

Many of these will provide a very natural fundraising ask, like, "Give today to make year 16 the best, yet!" or "Make a gift in honor of the Class of 2019."

You aren't limited to widely-recognized holidays or obvious milestones, either. You can create your own celebrations for donors to rally around.

For example, when charity: water provided clean water for 10 million people, they emailed everyone who had given in the past 13 years. They didn't limit the celebration to active or recent donors--they wanted to show that everyone was a part of reaching that moment.

Play 27 : Close the Loop and Show Impact

Donors give to make a difference, and it's up to nonprofits to show them that they've done it. Close every loop, and let donors know how the projects and programs they helped fund are going. Share your success stories, what you're learning, and the surprises that pop up along the way. Demonstrate how lives are changed and problems are solved, thanks to their gifts.

A great example of a responsive nonprofit in action is Watsi, an organization that helps fund healthcare around the world. They created a valentine (celebrate!) that highlights a supporter's impact, and introduces them to the people they're supporting.

When Watsi launched a new recurring gift option, The Universal Fund, they proceeded very carefully.

First, they listened. They added a checkbox to their donation form, and reached out to the first few hundred people who checked it, asking them to describe the concept of the Universal Fund in their own words. They used this language to launch the Fund, and connect with donors.

Then they kept listening as they connected, in order to make better suggestions. COO & Co-Founder, Grace Garey says, "For the longest time, we had it in our heads that people donate on Watsi because they are moved by a patient photo or story and they act on impulse. When we started to see droves of people sign up to donate continuously through the Universal Fund, we realized that users' motivations were really varied and there might be new ways to reach them we hadn't ever thought about."

Play 28 : Practice Gratitude

Before you make any suggestions, thank your donors. Communicating the impact of their donations and your gratitude is essential for showing that you consider them part of a community, not a walking wallet.

Thank your donors immediately and frequently. Your thank you messages should be timely, personal, specific and relevant. It's always a good time to thank your donors — you don't have to wait until they give again to say thanks.

Create a gratitude protocol that goes beyond a receipt and acknowledgment letter. Look to Food for the Hungry for a great example of using email to welcome and thank new donors.

Their new donor welcome email series features two thank you messages, along with several cultivation messages showing how their donation is being put to work. This creates several meaningful touch-points before they make another ask.

Making a gift is only the beginning of the relationship.

Conclusion:

Becoming A Responsive Fundraiser

When you become responsive instead of reactive, you'll connect with donors in a more meaningful way, adapt to the changes in the hyperconnected world, and grow your fundraising.

Using your responsive CRM, marketing automation, and data enrichment, combined with these Responsive Fundraising strategies, you can gain a deeper understanding of what your donors truly value and help them connect with your cause like never before.

Start responsive fundraising at your nonprofit.

Schedule your personalized demo of Virtuous today.

virtuouscrm.com/demo